The 5-Minute
Bible Study
Journal
For Women

This Journal Belongs To

_____

Copyright © 2024 by Cicilia Patrick

All rights reserved.

The publisher retains all rights. Reproduction or transmission of any part of this publication for commercial purposes is strictly prohibited, unless authorized in writing by the publisher. However, brief quotations in printed reviews are permitted with proper acknowledgement.

All scriptural excerpts are sourced from the New International Version (NIV), with the exception of a few. Any scriptural excerpts labeled MSG are sourced from The Message Bible translation.

Table of Contents

01 | His Chosen Ones Are Remembered and Redeemed

02. Four Centuries of Grace
03. The Silver Lining in Your Challenges
04. Take a Stand
05. Embrace the Faith of Jochebed
06. Miriam: A Helpful Daughter
07. Be a Batyah
08. The Consequences of Unchecked Anger
10. Stand Up for the Defenseless
11. Remember to Be Grateful
12. Bouncing From Failure
13. Here I Am. Send Me
14. Who Am I?
15. God's Promises Are Sure and Amen
16. What Is That in Your Hand?
17. The Rod: A Symbol of God's Authority
18. The Meaning of a Leprous Hand
19. Turning the Waters of the Nile Into Blood
20. Zipporah: A Supportive Wife
21. When God Hardens a Man's Heart
22. Never waste a Crisis
23. Redeemed Parents, Redeem Your Children
24. The Cloudy Leader
25. Are You Boxed in the Wilderness?
26. Do Not Be Afraid. Stand Firm
27. Your Path Led Through the Sea
28. The Song of Moses and the Lamb

29 | Redeemed, Provided For & Protected

30. The Miracle of Manna
31. Give Us THIS DAY Our Daily Manna
32. Is the Lord Among Us or Not?
33. Prayer and Hard Work Combo
34. Jehovah Nissi: The Lord Our Banner
35. Defend and Support the Vulnerable
36. The Gershom and Eliezer Moments
37. Success with Humility: True Mark of Greatness
38. Delegation: Unlocking the Power of Efficiency and Success
40. Unique Set of Qualities of a Great Leader
41. Saved unto Obedience
43. Sacred Ordinances for Eternal Salvation

44 | The Ten Commandments

45. The Decalogue
46. You Shall Have No Other God Before Me
48. You Shall Not Make Idols
49. You Shall Not Use God's Name in Vain
50. Let's Enjoy the Sabbath Rest
51. Honor Your Parents
52. You Shall Not Murder
53. You Shall Not Commit Adultery

- 54. You Shall Not Steal
- 55. You Shall Not Bear False Witness
- 56. You Shall Not Covet

58 | The Annual Feasts Of The Lord

- 59. Hope of Resurrection: The Day of the Firstfruits
- 60. Christ Our Passover Lamb Has Been Sacrificed
- 61. Get Rid of the Old Leaven of Wickedness
- 62. Pentecost

63 | The Sanctuary

- 65. The Ark of the Covenant
- 66. The Altar of Incense
- 67. The Menora
- 68. The Table of Showbread
- 69. The Lavar
- 70. The Altar of Burnt Offering

71 | Lessons From Mount Sinai and More

- 72. Let Go of Past Hurts
- 73. God of Justice and Mercy
- 74. Agreement Sealed in Blood
- 75. Urim and Thummim
- 76. Ear, Thumb and Big Toe
- 77. Skill Up
- 78. Choose God's Honor over Man's Approval
- 79. Own Up Aaron
- 80. Are You on the Lord's Side?
- 81. Prayer of a Righteous Woman
- 82. Time in the Closet Watching & Praying
- 84. The Power of Persistent Prayer
- 85. God's Character
- 86. Our Children May Harvest the Consequences of Our Actions
- 87. The Path to True Generosity: Unveiling the Principles of Giving
- 88. Diligent and Selfless Coworkers
- 89. Women Donated Brass Mirrors
- 90. Good Stewardship Is Exemplified by Accountability
- 91. God is Holy
- 92. Human Nature
- 93. Egypt Is a Precursor

Introduction

Hello Lovely Woman,

I guess you're juggling many things and it is not easy carving out time for Bible study. You can't add a thing to your to do list. Nevertheless, I believe you have a deep-seated desire to draw closer to God through consistent Bible study and prayers.

This book aims to assist you in four key areas. Firstly, it will aid you in initiating a consistent Bible Study routine. Secondly, it will prepare you for contributing positively to your community. I am confident that it will also motivate you to engage in daily prayer. Furthermore, it can support you in leading regular Bible studies for either a family or a church group.

In this book, I aim to trace the Exodus journey from Goshen to Mt. Sinai and offer concise reflections on key moments in the book of Exodus through a series of 85 impactful devotions. These devotions may be completed within a five-minute timeframe each day.

I have drawn a lot of inspiration from the following Bible verses:

"Man shall not live by bread alone, but by every word that comes from the mouth of God." Mat 4:4

"All Scripture is God-breathed and is useful for teaching, rebuking, correcting and training in righteousness, so that the servant of God may be thoroughly equipped for every good work." 2 Timothy 3:16-17

"Pray without ceasing" 1 Thessalonians 5:17

How to study the book:

Minute 1-2: Dive into a few selected verses taken from a passage the Bible books. If you have the time, explore the complete passage provided in every Bible study.

Minute 3-4: Immerse yourself in a concise devotion to gain a deeper understanding of the verse and receive valuable guidance on how to apply the profound teachings into your own life. Meditate on the devotion through the day.

Minute 5: Seek divine intervention by journaling a prayer in the space provided.

Devoting only five minutes every day to prayer and scripture has the potential to genuinely revolutionize your spiritual life.

Israelites Journey from Egypt to Mount Sinai

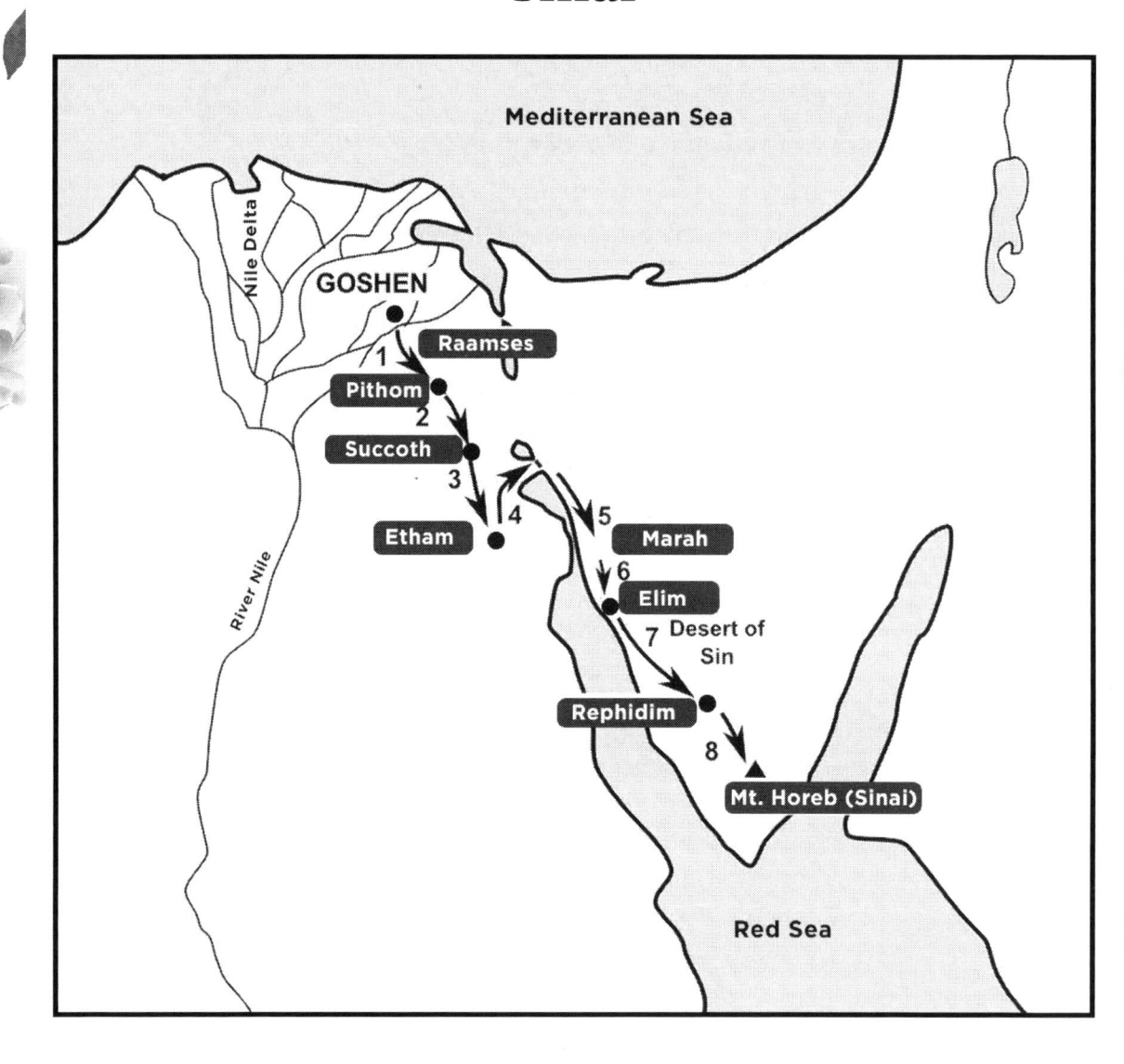

His Chosen Ones Are Remembered & Redeemed

Israel also came into Egypt,
And Jacob dwelt in the land of Ham.
He increased His people greatly,
And made them stronger than their enemies.
He turned their heart to hate His people,
To deal craftily with His servants.
He sent Moses His servant,
And Aaron whom He had chosen.
They performed His signs among them,
And wonders in the land of Ham.
He sent darkness, and made it dark;
And they did not rebel against His word.
He turned their waters into blood,
And killed their fish.
Their land abounded with frogs,
Even in the chambers of their kings.
He spoke, and there came swarms of flies,
And lice in all their territory.
He gave them hail for rain,
And flaming fire in their land.
He struck their vines also, and their fig trees,
And splintered the trees of their territory.
He spoke, and locusts came,
Young locusts without number,
And ate up all the vegetation in their land,
And devoured the fruit of their ground.
He also destroyed all the firstborn in their land,
The first of all their strength.

Psalms 105:23-36

Four Centuries of Grace

"Then the Lord said to him, "Know for certain that for four hundred years your descendants will be strangers in a country not their own and that they will be enslaved and mistreated there." Genesis 15:13

Have you ever wondered why slavery took four hundred years? A quick answer: He's a sovereign God who determines what to do with his creation. We can trust his actions because he is a just and a righteous God.

After four centuries, Israelites plundered Egypt and came out with great possession (Exodus 12:36). God ensured they were compesated fully in kind for their service of slavery. They needed resources to start, grow and develop the kingdom of Israel. The painful experience of bondage taught them patience and made them ready to accept the gift of redemption.

Also, during this four-hundred-year period, the Canaanites were on probation. God was patient with them to change their increasingly abominable conduct. If they remained unchanged throughout this period and continued in the life of sin, they would be ripe for God's judgment (Genesis 16:15). God had prepared an army of Israelites to bring His judgments to the Canaanites.

The four centuries attest that God is compassionate and gracious, slow to anger, abounding in love and faithfulness (Exodus 34:6)

Prayers:
....
....
....
....
....

The Silver Lining in Your Challenges

"Consider it pure joy, my brothers and sisters, whenever you face trials of many kinds, because you know that the testing of your faith produces perseverance. Let perseverance finish its work so that you may be mature and complete, not lacking anything."
James 1: 2-4, Exodus 1:8-14

For the four Centuries the Hebrews were in Egypt they enjoyed a longer period of growth and prosperity and a shorter period of slavery and adversity. The difficulty of slavery was a tool in God's hands to ready the Hebrews and make them willing to depart when a call was made.

Life on earth is not linear, sometimes we're enjoying a life of luxury and ease while at other times life becomes burdensome and dreary. To some, a life of ease and comfort can make them so attached to this world that they forget heaven, our final resting place.

The seasons of trouble and suffering should be taken as means of strengthening our commitment to God and loosening our grip on the things of this world. The God of bad times is the one of good times. Mountain tops are good but it is in the valleys that you can grow.

Prayers:

....
....
....
....
....

Take a Stand

" And because the midwives feared God, he gave them families of their own."
Exodus 1:21

Shiphrah and Puah were ordinary but God-fearing Hebrew young midwives who worked at an Egyptian birthing center. Aware of the consequences, they defied the King's edict to kill the Hebrew male newborns. They saved the life of baby Moses who grew up to save the Israelites from slavery. God honored the two midwives and blessed them with families of their own.

If you find yourself in a position of employment or influence and are faced with the temptation to act against God's will, humbly seek His guidance and strength to boldly stand up for what is right.

Prayers:

....
....
....
....
....
....
....
....
....
....
....

Embrace the Faith of Jochebed

" Now to him who is able to do immeasurably more than all we ask or imagine, according to his power that is at work within us, to him be glory in the church and in Christ Jesus throughout all generations, for ever and ever! Amen."
Ephesians 3:20-21, Exodus 2:1-10

Jochebed was an anxious expectant mother who was well aware of the consequences if her baby turned out to be a boy. She finally delivered a handsome baby boy. With great faith, she bravely defied Pharaoh's order and concealed the baby for three months. When she could not conceal the baby anymore, she crafted an ark of bulrushes, placed her baby in it and floated it on the bank of the Nile.

Jochebed had an inspired thought that the baby was an extraordinary child. She also had faith that somehow the God of their forefathers would save the baby according to His promises. This faith dispelled her fears and despair. This faith never exempted her from doing all within her means to save the baby. Even when she had exhausted her means, she gladly surrendered to God.

Her faith was sorely tested, but finally, God brought help from Pharaoh's daughter, an unlikely source, and kept the child safe. Jochebed was paid wages from the royalty for nursing her baby.

Notes:

....
....
....
....
....

Miriam: A Helpful Daughter

"Let us not become weary in doing good, for at the proper time we will reap a harvest if we do not give up."
Galatians 6:9, Exodus 2:3-10, Exodus 15:20-21

Miriam is an example of a helpful daughter. She stood with her mother in moments of anxiety to actively watch over the ark that bore her baby brother Moses on River Nile. She was clever to suggest her mother be a nurse to baby Moses. This allowed her family to earn wages from the royalty for taking care of their baby.

She is recognized in the bible as one of the three deliverers who played a vital role in the redemption of Israelites from slavery. On the shores of the Red Sea, she led a choir of women in singing and dancing praising God for the ultimate victory over Pharaoh and his elite soldiers.

A teenage girl should be an extra pair of hands in the home, helping her parents with housekeeping duties and other responsibilities. Like Miriam, they need encouragement in taking initiative and employing creativity in problem-solving. They will be prepared for leadership now and in the future.

Prayers:

....
....
....
....
....
....

Be a Batyah

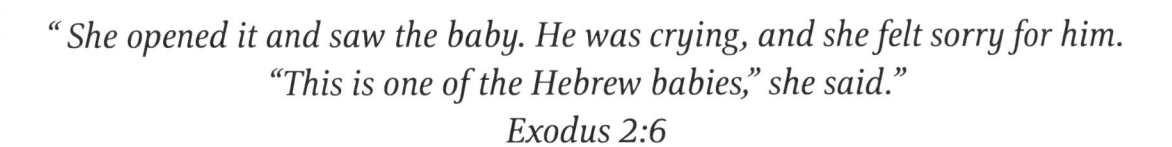

"She opened it and saw the baby. He was crying, and she felt sorry for him. "This is one of the Hebrew babies," she said."
Exodus 2:6

Upon opening the ark, Batyah, Pharaoh's daughter, was met with the sight of a weeping infant boy. Her heart was filled with empathy as she realized that the child was one of the Hebrew male newborns concealed from the Egyptian oppressors. Determined to provide for the baby's needs, Batyah arranged for a nurse and committed to covering the expenses of his care until he reached adulthood.

Batyah followed through. When the baby was fully grown, he was brought to her in the palace. She officially adopted him and named him Moses. He became a son of royalty. He was thereafter nourished, sheltered, clothed and educated as Pharaoh's son. She was one voice of reason against many unreasonable patriotic Egyptians. She went against her father and saved a baby.

Are you living in a community where racism, tribalism or marginalization prevail but you have not condemned it because it does not affect you? What can you do for people of color in your community who are victims of racial injustices? Join the minority and give the voice of reason against racism. Counter racist statements when you hear them. Do you have friends across the class divide?

Prayers:

....
....
....
....
....

The Consequences of Unchecked Anger

"In your anger do not sin: Do not let the sun go down while you are still angry, and do not give the devil a foothold." Ephesians 4:26-27, Exodus 2:11-12

Moses possessed remarkable qualities of a distinguished individual. However, there were instances where he demonstrated his fallibility, reminding us that he was merely human. At times, his anger overpowered his better judgment.

Out of anger, Moses killed an Egyptian and buried him in the sand. As a result of this hasty action, He was forced to flee the palace and he became a fugitive in Midian for forty years.

On another occasion, he was sorely upset by the murmuring and the bad attitude from the Israelites in their moments of want. Moses, instead of following God's instruction to speak to the rock, struck it twice with his rod. This action displeased God, and Moses did not step in Canaan.

Moses, also out of anger, dropped and broke the stones tablets containing God's law, when he descended from Mount Horeb and found the Israelites worshiping the golden calf.

When you're sorely upset and you're burning with anger, and you're about to take matters into your hands, take deep breaths until you're able to cool down. Always do this until you're able to control and sit on your anger. Pray to God to help you and He will.

Actions out of anger manifest a lack of faith in God's ability to intervene in a situation. It is the self rearing its ugly head and saying, "I can handle this better". Finally, anger hurts and derails God's work more than it promotes it. Always.

Prayers:

Stand Up for the Defenseless

"Now a priest of Midian had seven daughters, and they came to draw water and fill the troughs to water their father's flock. Some shepherds came along and drove them away, but Moses got up and came to their rescue and watered their flock." Exodus 2:16-17

This is a scenario that pits the daughters of Jethro against the rude sons of the wilderness. The sons of the wilderness had no patience to wait for their turn to draw water from the well and water their flock. They went further to use the water the daughters of Reul had drawn for their flock. They had made this a habit because, on the day Moses came to their help, they returned home early. The men who were supposed to defend their daughters are the same ones who ensured their rights were trampled upon.

Moses stood up and helped them. Though he was one man against many, he was bold and determined to stand in their way until the daughters watered their flock. We allow the strong to subvert the existing systems of justice and lord over the weak. Let's all become Moses and stand for their rights. Their labor will become easy and enjoyable. Let's become champions for the weak.

Prayers:

....
....
....
....
....
....
....
....

Remember to Be Grateful

"And where is he?" Reuel asked his daughters. "Why did you leave him? Invite him to have something to eat." Exodus 2:20

Reul's daughters returned so early that day. Moses courageously protected them against the impolite Midianite shepherds and helped them water their sheep.

Reul was a man of discernment and was concerned the daughters left a stranger who had been so kind to them at the well, stranded and unappreciated. Moses was called and in his home, he found hospitality, employment and a wife.

How many times, like Reul's daughters, the spirit of ingratitude gets the best of us? We forget those who were helpful and supportive the sooner we're out of danger.

Let's pray to God to grant us the spirit of gratitude. Remind us of those who have been kind to us and give us the ability to show them gratitude. Even in small ways.

Notes:

....
....
....
....
....
....
....
....

Bouncing From Failure

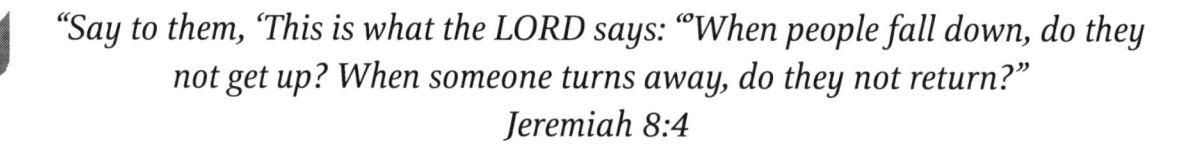

"Say to them, 'This is what the LORD says: "When people fall down, do they not get up? When someone turns away, do they not return?"
Jeremiah 8:4

In a remarkable display of unwavering loyalty, Moses consciously aligned himself with his own people, taking a stand against the injustice of slavery. However, when he killed an Egyptian, he came out as a man with good intentions trying to accomplish God's will by human abilities and wisdom.

He betrayed Pharaoh who consequently sought to have him killed. He had to flee for his life.

Through his exile, Moses traded the easy and luxurious life of the palace for the melancholic and difficult life of the wilderness.

In Midian, he felt all his choice and ambition of delivering the Hebrews from bondage had amounted to nought. The environment was not suitable for a man of his background and training. Life had become a disaster.

But as time went by he reconciled with his new situation, he laid aside the prince mentality and became a servant in Jethro's home until God came calling him to the duty of redeeming his people. God can use broken vessels for his ministry.

Prayers:

....
....
....
....
....

Here I Am. Send Me

"Then I heard the voice of the Lord saying, "Whom shall I send? And who will go for us?" And I said, "Here am I. Send me!" Isaiah 6:8, Exodus 3:1-4:17

At Mount Horeb, God appeared to Moses in the form of a burning bush and introduced Himself as the God of his forefathers. He revealed to him that he had seen the misery of the Israelites in slavery, had heard their cry and had come down to save them.

As the redeemed, God desires to use us as his instruments to redeem his people from the slavery of sin. The lust of the flesh, lust of the eyes and pride of life has left sinners weary, enslaved and miserable. Under Satan's taskmasters, they have long toiled in the fields of sin and they are now ready for an alternative lifestyle.

God can redeem them alone but He wants you to enjoy the blessings of working with him. Self-doubt, fear of rejection, fear of leaving our comfort zones and potential dangers of the calling have remained barriers.

Like Moses, God encourages us, don't fear, "My presence will be with you. Always. So Now Go".

Prayers:

....
....
....
....
....
....
....

Who Am I?

"But Moses said to God, "Who am I that I should go to Pharaoh and bring the Israelites out of Egypt?"" Exodus 3:11

Forty years back, Moses offered himself to save his people. They rejected him and called him an imposter. He fled to exile a disappointed man. Moses knew the Egyptian language and culture very well. He had stayed in the court and was highly trained and learned yet he felt the forty years of sheep-tending had downgraded his experience and rendered him unfit for the calling.

Diplomacy with Pharaoh, leading the princes and the Israelite congregation required someone with tongue power but Moses was slow of speech.

From his military training, Moses knew it was a tough task to redeem millions of unarmed slaves from a great civilization without a proper military plan.

A combination of these factors made Moses feel unfit for the calling. But God assured him of His presence through the mission. He gave him Aaron to help him in diplomacy.

Prayers:

....
....
....
....
....
....

God's Promises Are Sure and Amen

"For no matter how many promises God has made, they are "Yes" in Christ. And so through him the "Amen" is spoken by us to the glory of God. 1 Corinthians 1:20, Exodus 3:12

God's promises are as certain as the sunrise in the East. Just as He fulfilled His promise to Abraham after four hundred years, He will fulfill His promises to us as well. He delivered the Israelites from a life of slavery and mistreatment, leading them towards a future filled with hope in the promised land.

When Moses doubted God, He assured him the Jewish assembly would worship him on Mount Horeb on their way from Egypt. It came to pass.

We can trust God to guide us and provide us with perfect gifts, answering our flawed prayers. This promise is found in James 1:17.

The Bible is filled with countless divine promises, and we can rely on God to fulfill them in our lives.

Prayers:

....
....
....
....
....
....
....

What Is That in Your Hand?

Then the Lord said to him, "What is that in your hand?" "A staff," he replied.
Exodus 4:2

God can achieve great things through humble means. God put this question to Moses when he called him to the mission of saving the Israelites. Moses had a common staff with which he shepherded Jethro's sheep.

When he cast the rod down at God's command and took it back, God did something to it. He consecrated it and it became a special staff. With it, he made flies out of the dust, parted the red sea, won the battle with Amalekites and brought water out of the rock.

We can efficiently serve God in our diverse ordinary occupations. That's what we have in our hands. God instructs us to cast them at his feet, he will bless and consecrate them. When we pick them up, let us employ them to bring honor and glory to his name.

Prayers:

....
....
....
....
....
....
....

The Rod: A Symbol of God's Authority

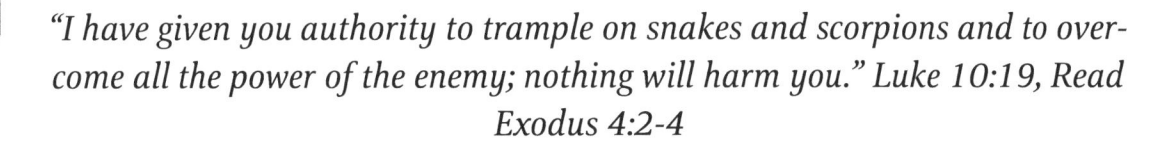

"I have given you authority to trample on snakes and scorpions and to overcome all the power of the enemy; nothing will harm you." Luke 10:19, Read Exodus 4:2-4

When Moses cast his rod on the ground and it changed into a venomous serpent, he felt very threatened. God commanded him to gather the courage and take the serpent by the tail, and the serpent changed back into a rod.

A serpent was a symbol that represented the power of the Egyptian monarch. The rod represented God's authority and with it, Moses was going to confront the Egyptian monarch to free the Israelites.

The monarch was as dangerous as the venomous snake, but the Lord assured Moses he would take them by the tail. With all their military and economic power, the monarch would be helpless before God.

Whatever danger we will face in doing God's work, his authority will help us overcome and nothing will harm us. Let's march forth with courage.

Prayers:

....
....
....
....
....

The Meaning of a Leprous Hand

"Then the Lord said, "Put your hand inside your cloak." So Moses put his hand into his cloak, and when he took it out, the skin was leprous —it had become as white as snow. Now put it back into your cloak," he said. So Moses put his hand back into his cloak, and when he took it out, it was restored, like the rest of his flesh." Exodus 4:6-7

God made Moses' hand white of leprosy and restored it thereafter to resemble the rest of the body. Leprosy was an incurable disease in those times. Leprosy represented slavery and the ill-treatment of God's people by Pharaoh's taskmasters. This sign proved God had endowed Moses with the authority to deliver Israelites from slavery.

God can bring judgment to those who refuse to obey his commands. He also promises mercy, forgiveness and restoration to the repentant.

Christ can deliver us from the slavery of sin. His death offers both hope to the repentant sinner and judgment to the unrepentant sinner.

Prayers:

....
....
....
....
....
....

Turning the Waters of the Nile Into Blood

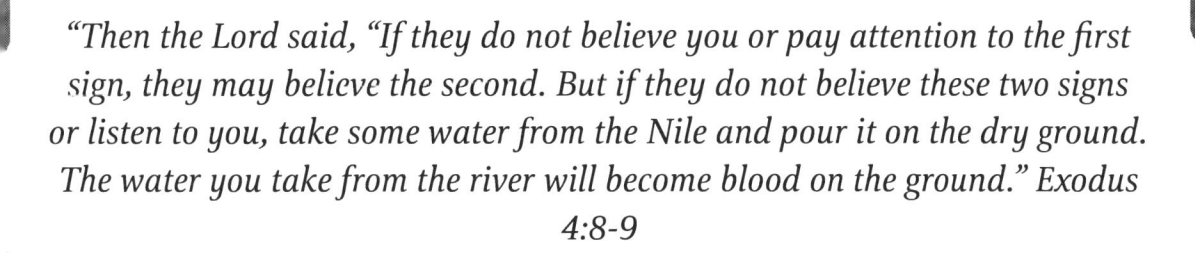

"Then the Lord said, "If they do not believe you or pay attention to the first sign, they may believe the second. But if they do not believe these two signs or listen to you, take some water from the Nile and pour it on the dry ground. The water you take from the river will become blood on the ground." Exodus 4:8-9

If Pharaoh would not believe the voice of the first two signs, God was willing to speak through the third: turning the waters of the River Nile into blood. The river was the source of their agricultural and economic prosperity, if you destroy it you destroy their livelihoods. The river was also a god to them.

This is evidence that God is patient with us and willing to provide an abundance of evidence to remove all doubt and unbelief from our lives.

The unbelief is punishable when we harden our hearts despite the evidence.

Prayers:

....
....
....
....
....
....
....
....
....

Zipporah: A Supportive Wife

"Now may the God of peace who brought again from the dead our Lord Jesus, the great shepherd of the sheep, by the blood of the eternal covenant, equip you with everything good that you may do his will, working in us[a] that which is pleasing in his sight, through Jesus Christ, to whom be glory forever and ever. Amen." Hebrews 13:20,21 Exodus 4:24-26

Zipporah is the Midianite wife Moses married while in exile. She's an example of women who are married to spouses across race and religion. Women who have to endure loneliness as their spouses are engaged in serving God in their leadership capacities.

It is also impressive how she handled ridicule from her in-laws with calmness.

When they lodged on their way to Egypt, an angel of God threatened to kill Moses because they had not circumcised their son according to the command God gave to Abraham. She took the initiative, circumcised her son and saved Moses' life.

God requires obedience from us. It is never late to admit our transgressions and seek God's forgiveness and comply with his dictates.

Married women should support and checkmate their spouses to ensure they walk according to God's will.

Prayers:

....

....

....

....

....

When God Hardens a Man's Heart

"When men refuse to love the truth and be saved, God sends them a powerful delusion to believe the lies and delight in wickedness. God will finally hold them accountable for refusing to believe the truth." 2 Thessalonians 2:9-12
Exodus 10:1,20,27

God hardened Pharaoh's heart. He repeatedly tells Moses that he would harden Pharaoh's heart and then miraculously deliver the Israelites. In Romans 9:17-19, the bible says God made Pharaoh the king over Egypt to use him to display his power and proclaim his name in all the earth.

Pharaoh also hardened his heart. Whenever he obtained relief from the plagues, it became a reason to cement his resolve not to let God's people free. From the onset, he questioned God's authority; "Who is the Lord that I should obey Him and let Israel go?" He also at some point admitted liability for causing the plagues on his people. If he had believed God at the first sign, God would have stopped further signs.

Prayers:

....
....
....
....
....
....
....
....
....

Never waste a Crisis

"And we know that in all things God works for the good of those who love him, who[a] have been called according to his purpose" Romans 8:28

The ten plagues visited upon Pharaoh and his people did not work to turn his heart to God, instead, they served to harden his heart. Whenever the Israelites were tempted, they resorted to murmuring and rebellion. The crises of the terrible wilderness clouded their judgment and they quickly forgot how God had miraculously led them out of Egypt.

Troubles neither remove our guilt nor change the moral condition of our hearts. But they are powerful means to turn our hearts to God in prayer. When Israelites were sorely weighed down by the afflictions of slavery in Egypt, they began to pray and God heard their cry and came to their rescue.

Are you currently afflicted? That's an opportunity, don't waste it. Be patient, humble yourself under the mighty hand of God and pray. In due season, He will lift you up.

Prayers:

....
....
....
....
....
....
....
....
....

Redeemed Parents, Redeem Your Children

When you enter the land that the Lord will give you as he promised, observe this ceremony. And when your children ask you, 'What does this ceremony mean to you?' then tell them, 'It is the Passover sacrifice to the Lord, who passed over the houses of the Israelites in Egypt and spared our homes when he struck down the Egyptians.' Exodus 12:25-26

God assured the Hebrew adults they would finally enjoy life as redeemed parents in the promised land. He commanded them to remember to keep observing the Passover ordinance with an understanding of its significance in their redemption.

He also instructed them to use the ordinance as an opportunity to teach the curious minds of their children who would seek to understand its meaning. Parents were to respond to their children with precision according to God's word.

God is interested in our children just as he was interested in the Israelites' children. As the redeemed people, we're also called to be redeeming parents. Your children are looking up to you as an example of the adults they would be. Remember to mold your actions, character and mannerisms after God's word, and when they ask you the reason for your faith, refer them to God's word.

Timothy learned from the faith of his mother Eunice and his grandmother Lois, the foundation upon which Paul built to influence him into greatness in God's ministry.

Prayers:

....

....

....

....

....

The Cloudy Leader

"By day the Lord went ahead of them in a pillar of cloud to guide them on their way and by night in a pillar of fire to give them light, so that they could travel by day or night. " Exodus 13:21

The pillar of cloud and the pillar of fire were a sign of God's presence with the Istraelites throughout their journey in the wilderness. The pillar of cloud would shield them from the blistering sun of the wilderness while the pillar of fire would light their paths and provide them with warmth at night.

When the pillar of cloud advanced, it was time for them to break camp and advance, when it stopped, they would pitch their tents and rest.

The cloudy pillar led them to dangerous places that threatened their lives. In the same way, God is with us day and night to ensure our comfort, safety and security.

When his providence leads us to situations and places of trouble and affliction, we can trust him to make a way out.

Prayers:

....
....
....
....
....
....
....
....

Are You Boxed in the Wilderness?

"For Pharaoh will say of the Israelites, 'They are wandering the land in confusion; the wilderness has boxed them in." Exodus 14:3

The Israelites had a clean escape from bondage in Egypt. They were out of Pharaoh's sight but not forgotten. They were a free human resource who had immensely contributed to the prosperity of his kingdom. As they advanced from Egypt, they came to a desert area between the Nile Valley and the Red Sea where Pharaoh thought they had either lost their way or had gotten their Geography wrong. Here Pharaoh saw an opportunity and said, "I will pursue, I will overtake, I will divide the spoils; my lust shall be satisfied upon them; I will draw my sword, my hand shall destroy them". He forgot it was God who led them there.

Satan is more interested in new converts. He pursues them as they are celebrating victory over the life of sin and addictions, to confuse them and make them doubt their newfound faith. He knows he has half a chance to re-enslave them before they make their reformation firm through experience.

Prayers:

....
....
....
....
....
....
....
....
....
....

Do Not Be Afraid. Stand Firm

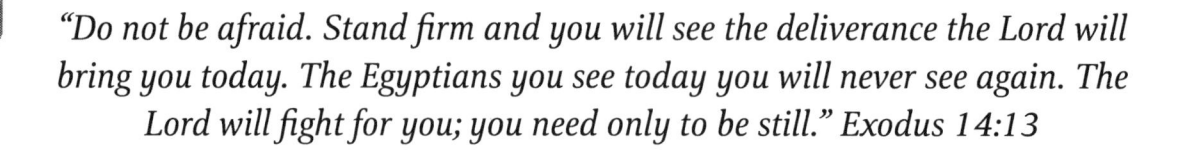

"Do not be afraid. Stand firm and you will see the deliverance the Lord will bring you today. The Egyptians you see today you will never see again. The Lord will fight for you; you need only to be still." Exodus 14:13

Israelites were shut in and there was no way of escape. Pharaoh's elite army was quickly catching up with them. Pharaoh had vowed to put them to the sword. Israelites had numbers against an army of six hundred soldiers, but they were unarmed, untrained and not battle-hardened.

They were sorely afraid, restless and desperate. In this moment they remembered to cry unto the Lord for help. The Lord answered their prayers though mingled with complaints.

God through Moses commanded them not to be afraid but stand firm.

There are situations where we must do something to help ourselves. But in other situations where we are out of our depth, we must surrender all to God. In our helpless moments, it is also our duty to quiet our timid hearts, patiently and courageously wait upon God's promises.

Hold your peace, and let the Lord fight for you.

Prayers:

....
....
....
....
....

Your Path Led Through the Sea

"Your path led through the sea, your way through the mighty waters, though your footprints were not seen." Psalms 77:19, Exodus 14:19-31

God wrought miracles to enable Israelites to pass through the Red Sea. The Egyptian army could not catch up with Israel and they finally perished in the waters of the sea.

He caused a wind to blow from the east and part the waters of the Red Sea to make a way for the Israelites.

God moved the pillar of cloud from the front to the rear to light the path for the Israelites and darken the one for the trailing Egyptian army.

Before dawn, when the army was way into the sea, God jammed the wheels of the chariots, and he caused terror and confusion among them. They attempted to escape back but it was too little too late, they all perished.

God can make a way where there seems to be none. We can trust God to protect us against our enemies or danger. The wiles and schemes of the devil are not a match to God's power to save.

When in doubt, we can rely on God's word to illuminate our decision-making and point us to the right paths.

Prayers:

....

....

....

The Song of Moses and the Lamb

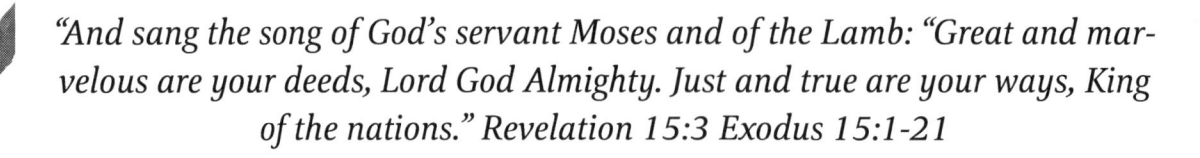

"And sang the song of God's servant Moses and of the Lamb: "Great and marvelous are your deeds, Lord God Almighty. Just and true are your ways, King of the nations." Revelation 15:3 Exodus 15:1-21

When the Israelites crossed the Red Sea, Moses composed a song of praise to God for the victory against Pharaoh and his army. With timbrels in their hands, women joined in dance and jubilation celebrating their glorious triumph.

The book of Revelation gives us a teaser of the events that will precede our escape from the earth on Christ's second coming. Those who would have obtained victory over sin will stand by the sea of glass mingled with fire, God will place harps in their hands, and they will sing the song of Moses, and the lamb through whom they were victorious.

For those on the Lord's side, victory is assured through Christ the lamb of God who was slain for our sins.

Prayers:

....
....
....
....
....
....
....
....
....

Redeemed, Provided For & Protected

He rebuked the Red Sea also, and it dried up;
So He led them through the depths,
As through the wilderness.
He saved them from the hand of him who hated them,
And redeemed them from the hand of the enemy.
The waters covered their enemies;
There was not one of them left.
Then they believed His words;
They sang His praise.

Psalms 106:9-12

He also brought them out with silver and gold,
And there was none feeble among His tribes.
Egypt was glad when they departed,
For the fear of them had fallen upon them.
He spread a cloud for a covering,
And fire to give light in the night.
The people asked, and He brought quail,
And satisfied them with the bread of heaven.
He opened the rock, and water gushed out;
It ran in the dry places like a river.

Psalms 105:37-41

The Miracle of Manna

"Then the Lord said to Moses, "I will rain down bread from heaven for you. The people are to go out each day and gather enough for that day. In this way I will test them and see whether they will follow my instructions."
Exodus 16:4

Camping in the wilderness of SIN was a season of greatest want. They had water but no food. The reserves of food they had had probably run out. They were weary and in need of refreshments after long treks in the desert.

This situation made them see some good from a disastrous past in Egypt and they forgot the promise of a better future in Canaan. They despaired and grumbled against God and He miraculously provided them with Manna.

They called Manna "what is it" because it was strange food to them. From that point, until some of them entered Canaan, a period of forty years, they received a constant supply of Manna every morning.

Each person was supposed to collect enough Manna for a day. Those who out of greed were tempted to keep the surplus for another day, it got spoiled. God was teaching them to take one day at a time and to depend on Him daily for their needs.

Manna was freely provided for, but men had a role to timely collect the manna and cook before eating. In the same way, God provides opportunities, but it is upon us to go out and exploit them to our benefit.

Prayers:

....

....

....

Give Us THIS DAY Our Daily Manna

"Give us today our daily bread."
Matthew 6:11, Exodus 16:18

The slow, the weak, the children, the elderly or the nursing mothers could not collect any or enough manna. God instructed Israelites to share the surplus for the benefit of those. This partly ensured everyone had enough share of manna for a day and partly ensured there were no wastages.

Give US TODAY OUR DAILY BREAD is a line in the Lord's prayers. It is OUR daily bread, not MY daily bread.

Over and above what we need for a day is for our needy neighbors.
Let us be kind and loving to one another. It's God's means of overcoming selfishness and greed.

Prayers:

....
....
....
....
....
....
....
....
....
....

Is the Lord Among Us or Not?

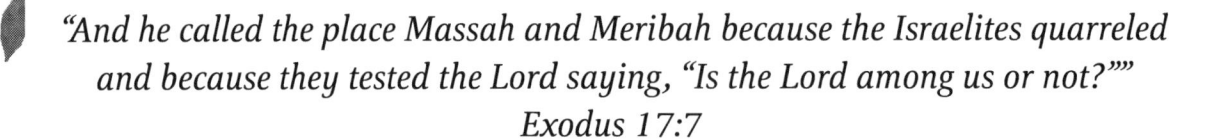

"And he called the place Massah and Meribah because the Israelites quarreled and because they tested the Lord saying, "Is the Lord among us or not?""
Exodus 17:7

At Marah, they found an oasis whose water was too bitter for drinking. Elim was fine, they found twelve wells for water and seventy palm trees for comfort. In the Desert of Sin, they lacked food. At Rephidim, they had manna but they could not find water for themselves and their animals. They were sorely tempted, they felt God had abandoned them to die of thirst. They became wild, they almost stoned Moses.

We all come to Rephidim. A place we expect to rest from the challenges of yesterday or past years but we're presented with new worse difficulties. We doubt God's presence which should presumably shield us from any challenges. We wrongly conclude that the Lord is not with us, we are on our own. God's tokens of grace and providence in the past have not worked faith in our lives.

They were wrong. In the porous rock of Rephidim, God had trapped volumes of water contained in an impervious layer of crust long before they arrived. When Moses struck this rock with his rod before the elders, plenty of water gushed out.

This proved God was among them, He was an ever-present help in times of need. In this temptation, he provided a way of escape.

Prayers:

....
....
....

Prayer and Hard Work Combo

"The Amalekites came and attacked the Israelites at Rephidim. Moses told Joshua, "Choose some of our men and go out to fight the Amalekites. Tomorrow I will stand on top of the hill with the staff of God in my hands."
Exodus 17:8-9

The Amalekite desert warriors attacked the Israelites while they journeyed to the promised land. They specifically targeted the weary and worn-out laggards. Moses instructed Joshua to assemble an army of able men and ready them to fight the Amalekites the following day. The army waged a day-long battle against the Amalekites while Moses, Aaron and Hur remained on the hill lifting God's staff. The fighting by Joshua's army and the lifting of the rod was done simultaneously until the Amalekites were all put to the sword.

It is conceivable that Satan may have taken control of your path towards achieving your objectives, resulting in you being trapped in a stagnant state. Are you interested in excelling academically, engaging in volunteer work, initiating or reinvigorating your professional journey, establishing and maintaining a fitness regimen, or embracing a new hobby? In that case, the rod of prayer and the sword of determination will assist you in overcoming this stagnant phase.

Notes:

....

....

....

....

....

....

Jehovah Nissi: The Lord Our Banner

"And Moses built an altar and named it 'The LORD is my Banner."
-Exodus 17:15

At Rephidim, God's people were called to fight against experienced Amalekite desert bandits. Through the concerted effort of Hur, Aaron and Moses in lifting God's staff, God intervened and delivered victory to an inexperienced and ill-equipped army of ex-slaves.

The rod of Moses was the Lord's banner under which the Israelites fought. Jehovah Nissi directed, aided and strengthened the Jewish army against the Amalekites.

Moses built an altar and called it "The Lord is my Banner" which means "Jehovah Nissi" in Hebrew.

As Christians, our battle is unlike the one against the Amalekites, "For our struggle is not against flesh and blood, but against the rulers, against the authorities, against the powers of this dark world and the spiritual forces of evil in the heavenly realms."

Jehovah-Nissi will ensure we triumph. Let's fight under His banner.

Prayers:

....
....
....
....
....
....

Defend and Support the Vulnerable

"When the Lord your God gives you rest from all the enemies around you in the land he is giving you to possess as an inheritance, you shall blot out the name of Amalek from under heaven. Do not forget!"
Deuteronomy 25:19, Exodus 17:8-16

The victory against the Amalekites at Rephidim was the beginning of God's Judgment against them for attacking the Israelites, especially the weak and the vulnerable. God reminds Israelites that once they possess Canaan, they should remember to wage war against the Amalekites from generation to generation until they are completely eliminated from the face of the earth.

This is a harsh verdict because the feeble, marginalized, impoverished, homeless, and defenseless hold a special place in the heart of God. Any act of aggression or unfairness towards them is a direct affront to God.

By demonstrating compassion, engaging in charitable acts, and making personal sacrifices, women have the ability to provide relief to those who are vulnerable. Can God rely on you?

Prayers:

....
....
....
....
....
....

The Gershom and Eliezer Moments

"And her two sons. One son was named Gershom, for Moses said, "I have become a foreigner in a foreign land"; and the other was named Eliezer, for he said, "My father's God was my helper; he saved me from the sword of Pharaoh." Exodus 18:3-4

Moses had two sons: Gershom and Eleazer. Gershom means I have been a stranger in a foreign land while Eleazer means the God of my fathers was my help. The two names capture the mood of Moses while in the wilderness of Midian and the other after he had triumphantly delivered the Israelites from slavery in Egypt.

For Christians like Moses, we are all Gershoms in this world, we have no abiding city here, we're homeless. Our citizenship is in heaven. This is the hope that should give us the grace to endure the challenges of our pilgrimage. When our Helper comes, He will take us home according to the promise.

In the patches of our life when our summer turns to winter, let's patiently wait for the Eliezer moment. It came for Moses, it will come for you, however long.

Prayers:

....
....
....
....
....
....
....
....

Success with Humility: True Mark of Greatness

"So Moses went out to meet his father-in-law and bowed down and kissed him. They greeted each other and then went into the tent." Exodus 18:7

"In the same way, you who are younger, submit yourselves to your elders. All of you, clothe yourselves with humility toward one another, because, "God opposes the proud but shows favor to the humble." 1 Peter 5:5

Moses had transformed a great deal since he left Midian at God's command to deliver the Israelites. A humble shepherd of Midian had grown to be a great leader of the millions. He rubbed shoulders with Pharaoh and his empire until they regarded him as a god. He oversaw great miracles that God performed to deliver the Hebrews, especially the crossing of the Red Sea and the drowning of the elite Egyptian army. His fame had gone far and wide.

On their way to Mount Sinai, his father-in-law paid them a courtesy call. He brought with him Moses' wife and children. Moses affectionately received his father-in-law, he bowed down and kissed him and took him to the tent where they reminisced. Later when Jethro gave him advice on how to better conduct his leadership, he took it with humility and implemented it.

Success, if it gets into one's head, can turn relationships on their head. Men who were initially warm, affectionate and friendly could turn cold, frozen and indifferent towards those they consider a level below them. Be humble.

Prayers:

....
....
....
....

Delegation: Unlocking the Power of Efficiency and Success

"This is not good!" Moses' father-in-law exclaimed. "You're going to wear yourself out—and the people, too. This job is too heavy a burden for you to handle all by yourself."
Exodus 18:17-18

During his stay, Jethro keenly observed how Moses tirelessly toiled from dawn till dusk, presiding over the cases brought by the Israelites. Regardless of his relentless efforts, Moses found it challenging to cope with the ever-increasing workload. This burden weighed heavily on him, leading to discontent among the masses due to the delayed resolution of their cases.

Jethro offered free advice. He told Moses to find able men, men of integrity and teach them to share this responsibility with him. Moses took this advice and created a hierarchical system that ensured only the difficult cases were escalated to him.

The outcome? The camp became like a well-oiled machine. The princes were happy to share the responsibility. Cases were timely resolved. Moses had time to spare for other responsibilities like writing the law and everybody was happy.

Are you currently having a lot more in your hands than you can handle? Carefully select what you can delegate. Identify able persons whom you can share the load with. Guide and instruct them on what to do and let them do it. You will be happy you did.

The church, the body of Christ with members who are diversely gifted should be efficient and it is not perfect until every member occupies their space and contributes to its perfection.

Prayers:

Unique Set of Qualities of a Great Leader

"But select capable men from all the people—men who fear God, trustworthy men who hate dishonest gain—and appoint them as officials over thousands, hundreds, fifties and tens." Exodus 18:21

Jethro gave an inspired counsel to Moses on the qualities of men for the office of assistant Judges. These qualities apply to God's people who are called to different positions of leadership in our times. Primarily, we are leaders of ourselves.

Able. This is our capacity to deliver in the leadership responsibilities. Few are born with leadership capacity. Many others have to grow their capacity for leadership through experience or training.

Love the truth. Seek to know the truth from the Bible. Scriptures are adequate to make one wise. Let's apply ourselves to their study. Pray to God for the willpower to profess and live the truth.

Fear God. We're God's steward and he entrusts us with leadership responsibilities. We should always subject ourselves to his Lordship. We need to have our eyes single on pleasing him.

Hate covetousness. There's always a temptation to undermine justice for personal gain. We've been called to high standards of integrity. We need to grow our hate for the vice and stand for justice.

Prayers:

....

....

Saved unto Obedience

"You yourselves have seen what I did to Egypt, and how I carried you on eagles' wings and brought you to myself. Now if you obey me fully and keep my covenant, then out of all nations you will be my treasured possession. Although the whole earth is mine, you will be for me a kingdom of priests and a holy nation." Exodus 19:4-6

It is a marvel how God sustained and cared for millions of people through a terrible and dangerous desert. The Bible tells us that He guarded them as the apple of his eye. He stirred their comfortable nest at Goshen and eventually brought them to the insecurities of the wilderness.

But like an eagle, he always hovered over the Israelites and carried them on his wings to places of safety whenever they felt threatened.

At Mount Sinai, God through Moses proposes to get into a covenant with his redeemed people. He required thorough obedience to his laws and fidelity to the covenant, not a mere profession of faith.

They needed to apply themselves to understanding his will and live accordingly. In return, God promised to treasure them above any other nation on earth. They would become a kingdom of priests and a holy nation to proclaim his greatness to other nations.

"But you are a chosen people, a royal priesthood, a holy nation, God's special possession, that you may declare the praises of him who called you out of darkness into his wonderful light." 1 Peter 2:9

Prayers:

Sacred Ordinances for Eternal Salvation

"They were all baptized into Moses in the cloud and in the sea. They all ate the same spiritual food and drank the same spiritual drink; for they drank from the spiritual rock that accompanied them, and that rock was Christ." 1 Corinthians 10:2-3

Moses was their redeemer. They were baptized into Moses because he was the go-between the Israelites and God. Were it not for Moses, none of the Hebrews would have escaped Egypt. In this manner, Jesus is our mediator, none will be saved except through and by him. He saved us and he is now interceding for us.

The Israelites were baptized in the waters of the Red Sea. The descending and ascending from the waters were symbolic of their baptism. They buried the old nature of slavery and were resurrected into a new life of freedom and hope. The pillar cloud over their heads was emblematic of the presence of God.

The Israelites broke bread and drank from the cup. Their eating of manna and water from the rock was akin to the last supper that Jesus had with his disciples when he broke bread and gave them a drink. He commanded Christians to observe this ceremony to commemorate his death and as a promise of his return.

Do you believe in the redemption work of Jesus Christ? Be baptized, and as often as you can participate in the holy communion.

Prayers:

....

....

....

The Ten Commandments

For He remembered His holy promise,
And Abraham His servant.
He brought out His people with joy,
His chosen ones with gladness.
He gave them the lands of the Gentiles,
And they inherited the labor of the nations,
That they might observe His statutes
And keep His laws.
Praise the LORD!

Psalms 105:42-45

The Decalogue

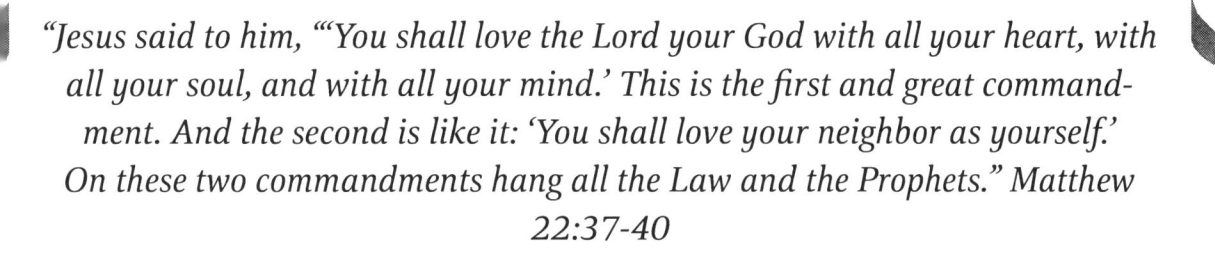

"Jesus said to him, '"You shall love the Lord your God with all your heart, with all your soul, and with all your mind.' This is the first and great commandment. And the second is like it: 'You shall love your neighbor as yourself.' On these two commandments hang all the Law and the Prophets." Matthew 22:37-40

The ten commandments are an executive summary expressing God's will. The mosaic law, the words of the prophets and the teachings in the new testament all find their convergence in the ten commandments.

One tablet had the first four commandments, while the other had the remaining six. They together express how man should relate to God and how man should relate to man.

God deserves and claims our sincere love, we need to love Him with our lips and with our actions. Second to this love is the love for fellow human beings; it confirms our love for God.

Christ summarized the ten commandments into two. First, love the Lord your God with all your heart and with all your soul and with all your mind. Second, love your neighbor as yourself.

Sincere, true, noble love for all men springs from the true love of God.

Prayers:

....
....
....
....

You Shall Have No Other Gods Before Me

" Moses possessed remarkable qualities of a distinguished individual. However, there were instances where he demonstrated his fallibility, reminding us that he was merely human. At times, his anger overpowered his better judgment."
Ephesians 3:20-21

Israelites were tempted to worship Baal and other gods for what they promised. Baal god for instance promised fertility and prosperity. Baal was a creation of the Canaanites whose worship involved prostitution and child sacrifice.

As believers, it is our divine duty to wholeheartedly embrace and obey God's laws. He desires us to stand out from the crowd, to be peculiar in our devotion to Him. Our hearts should be filled with a genuine longing to love and be loved by our Heavenly Father.

However, when we allow our pursuits for power, fame, sex, or money to take precedence over God's will, we unknowingly jeopardize His supreme position in our lives. These worldly desires become idols, replacing the true God who deserves our unwavering devotion.

Let us remember that true fulfillment lies in aligning our lives with God's purpose and surrendering our desires to His divine plan. By doing so, we not only honor Him but also find genuine joy, peace, and contentment that can only come from a life lived in obedience to our loving Creator.

"No one can serve two masters. Either you will hate the one and love the other, or you will be devoted to the one and despise the other. You cannot serve both God and money" Mat 6:24

Prayers:

You Shall Not Make Idols

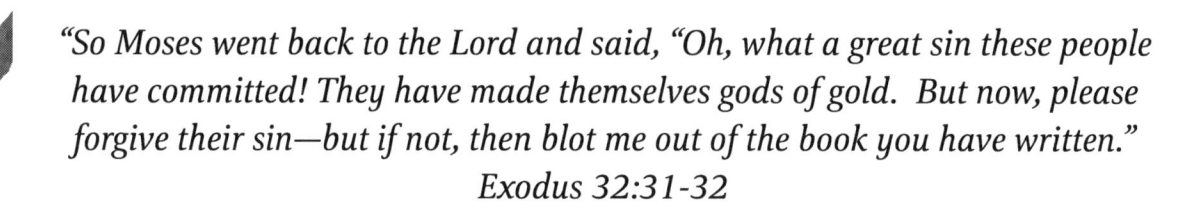

"So Moses went back to the Lord and said, "Oh, what a great sin these people have committed! They have made themselves gods of gold. But now, please forgive their sin—but if not, then blot me out of the book you have written."
Exodus 32:31-32

It is a common temptation for us to idolize the things we create and achieve through our own efforts. Whether it is material wealth, advanced technology, or luxurious homes, we often believe that these things can fulfill our desires and ambitions. We invest our time, energy, and resources into obtaining and maintaining them, sometimes forgetting the importance of our faith in God.

However, it is crucial to remember that this commandment prohibits the worship of any form of idol or image. Instead, we should prioritize our worship towards God and trust in His guidance for our lives.

Prayers:

....
....
....
....
....
....
....
....

You Shall Not Use God's Name in Vain

"You shall not misuse the name of the Lord your God, for the Lord will not hold anyone guiltless who misuses his name." Exodus 20:7

God cares about his reputation, and as his children, it is our duty to honor and respect his name. As followers of Christ, we are his representatives on earth, and our behavior and actions reflect either glory or disgrace upon God's holy name.

When we deliberately disobey his commandments, we distort his image and disrespect his name. Marriage vows are legitimized in God's name. When we fail to keep the promises in the vows, we dishonor his name.

We must refrain from using his name to defame others or to justify our own choices and behaviors. Instead, let us refrain from invoking his name inappropriately.

Sometimes, we may believe that we understand God's intentions in his dealings with people, but we must be cautious not to misuse his name in doing so.

Prayers:

....
....
....
....
....
....
....
....

Let's Enjoy the Sabbath Rest

"So the Son of Man is Lord even of the Sabbath." Mark 2:28

Sabbath rest is among the ten commandments God wrote with his finger making it a perpetually binding law. God instituted the Sabbath at creation. On the seventh day, God rested from his labors, and he blessed this day and made it holy. Even before the giving of the moral law, the Jews observed the Sabbath.

The new testament reminds us God created the Sabbath for the benefit of man. It is a time to rest, heal and replenish one's energies after six days of Labour. It is also a day to reconnect with God, our creator and redeemer, through acts of worship. It's a day when all, including servants and beasts of burden, are to experience the freedom of redemption.

To the Israelites, the Sabbath was a perpetual sign between them and God. Through its observance, they would know Him as the Lord who consecrates them.

Let us enjoy the physical and spiritual rest in Christ, the Lord of the Sabbath, who can sanctify and make us holy.

Six days of work are as important as the Sabbath. When we diligently work and render our services during the week, we're obeying the Sabbath command.

For our economic prosperity, we don't need seven days of work, we can trust in God's provision and enjoy the Sabbath rest.

Prayers:

....

....

....

Honor Your Parents

"Honor your father and your mother, so that you may live long in the land the Lord your God is giving you" Exodus 20:12

To honor our parents means that our speech, actions and attitudes should always be gracious to them. We should always seek opportunities to show them support, affection and gratitude. Kids are required to be obedient to their parents in the Lord.

In the Bible, children were supposed to take care of their parents in their sunset days. It is also our responsibility to ensure our parents are comfortable in their old days.

Even if you have been a victim of unfair treatment from your parents, you're not exonerated from the responsibility to respect them. Reconcile with them, seek their approval and you will prosper.

Prayers:

....
....
....
....
....
....
....
....
....

You Shall Not Murder

"You shall not murder." Exodus 20:13

Accidents and homicides are among the top causes of death in the world. God warned against intentionally taking the life of another man. We should seek and advocate non-violent ways of resolving personal or political conflicts.

We need to guard against errors of commission or omission that lead to the loss of lives. We have an obligation as God's children to work towards safety in our homes and workplaces. Keep poison, inflammable and drugs out of the reach of children. Ensure dogs are leashed in public places. Let us take measures to avoid road accidents.

Anger is a violation of this commandment especially as it leads to sinful actions. We should not brood over anger for long periods but seek the earliest opportunity to reconcile with our offenders.

Prayers:

You Shall Not Commit Adultery

"You shall not commit adultery." Exodus 20:14

God instituted marriage as a holy institution at creation. Adultery is a sin against God as it fragments the God-ordained covenant between husband and wife. Sex also is a God-given gift that should be enjoyed within the confines of a marriage institution.

As we guard against the actual act of adultery, with the help of God, we need to work towards purity of mind because that's where adultery is conceived before it is expressed physically.

It is crucial for us to establish secure boundaries and strive to function within those boundaries. In professional settings, it is important to maintain a friendly and kind demeanor towards everyone, while also remaining vigilant against unnecessary familiarity. Decline or reschedule invitations to odd-hour meetings.

As much as possible, married people should not spend too much time away from their spouses.

Parents should be exemplary to their children on matters of sexual purity.

Prayers:

....
....
....
....
....

You Shall Not Steal

"You shall not steal." Exodus 20:15

Stealing is a grave offense that deprives individuals of the fruits of their hard work. It is an act of dishonesty and a shortcut for those who are unwilling to put in the effort and patiently wait for the rewards of their labor.

There are various ways in which stealing occurs, ranging from directly stealing from one's colleagues or employees to misusing available resources for personal gain.

In the business world, some resort to deception, spreading false information or manipulating prices to secure sales or increase market share. Such practices not only cheat customers out of their money but also fail to meet their expectations.

Exploiting someone's vulnerabilities, fears, or powerlessness without their voluntary consent is morally wrong.

It is essential to uphold integrity and refrain from stealing, whether it be withholding the tithe from God or engaging in laziness at work, as it ultimately amounts to stealing from one's employer.

Prayers:

....
....
....
....
....
....

You Shall Not Bear False Witness

"You shall not give false testimony against your neighbor." Exodus 20:16

Refrain from speaking ill of others behind their backs or participating in discussions that misrepresent or slander individuals. Instead, choose not to tarnish someone's reputation without evidence or the opportunity for them to defend themselves.

Similarly, refrain from negative campaigns that seek to undermine the credibility of your competition in front of your audience.

Be cautious of disguising slander as prayer requests or pastoral concerns.

When someone is defamed, we end up tarnishing our own reputation as well. Instead, address any issues or concerns directly with the person involved.

Prayers:

....
....
....
....
....
....
....
....
....
....

You Shall Not Covet

"You shall not covet your neighbor's house. You shall not covet your neighbor's wife, or his male or female servant, his ox or donkey, or anything that belongs to your neighbor." Exodus 20:17

Covetousness is a strong wish to have your neighbors' possessions. It is a desire that results from an unhealthy comparison between what you own against what a neighbor owns, which leaves you less content with your possessions. Your neighbor may become an object of envy and hate which ultimately affects how you relate with them.

If you strongly desire your neighbor's spouse, you will begrudge yours, and it might lead you to infidelity.

Covetousness may breed resentment against God. You will grow feelings that God is biased in His dealings with the affairs of men. It robs you of joy and peace of mind leaving you miserable.

Pray God to grant you a spirit of contentment. Count your blessings, name them one by one and it will surprise you what the Lord has done. You will always admire something in other people's lives. People will always find something going for you. Let's learn to love our neighbors for who they are. Let's celebrate their God-given strengths and blessings.

"But godliness with contentment is great gain. For we brought nothing into the world, and we can take nothing out of it. But if we have food and clothing, we will be content with that." 1 Tim 6:6-8

Prayers:

The Annual Feasts of the Lord

SUNDAY	MONDAY	TUESDAY	WEDNESDAY	THURSDAY	FRIDAY	SATURDAY
						1
2	3	4	5	6	7	8
9	10 *The passover lamb is set aside & observed for defects*	11	12	13	14 *Spices are brought Jesus the passover lamb dies at 3pm (between two evenings)*	15 *1st day of the week of unleavened bread The Sabbath. Jesus rests in the tomb*
16 *Day of the first fruts Jesus resurrects*	17	18	19	20	21	22
23	24	25	26	27	28	20
30						

Three times a year you are to celebrate a festival to me. Celebrate the Festival of Unleavened Bread; for seven days eat bread made without yeast, as I commanded you. Do this at the appointed time in the month of Aviv, for in that month you came out of Egypt. No one is to appear before me empty-handed. Celebrate the Festival of Harvest with the firstfruits of the crops you sow in your field. Celebrate the Festival of Ingathering at the end of the year, when you gather in your crops from the field. Three times a year all the men are to appear before the Sovereign Lord. *Exodus 23: 14-17*

Hope of Resurrection: The Day of the Firstfruits

"The graves opened, and many of God's people who had died were raised from the dead. They came out of the graves after Jesus was raised from the dead and went into the holy city, where they appeared to many people. Matthew" 27:51-52

The Day of the Firstfruits was done on the 16th day of the week of unleavened bread or the third day of the Passover week.

The Hebrews brought the heads of grains to the sanctuary and the priest would take a handful of them and wave them to the Lord before the golden altar. This was a sign of thanksgiving and praise to God for the harvest.

After His burial, Christ was resurrected on the third day, which coincided with the day of the first fruits, as a pledge of resurrection to those who will believe in Him.

Many saints who had died rose from the graves with Jesus Christ and Christ presented these handful of saints before God in the heavenly sanctuary as a pledge of the final harvest on his return.

Our faith as Christians is founded on life after death. Through this festival, Jesus proved the concept of resurrection beyond any reasonable doubt.

Prayers:

....
....
....
....

Christ Our Passover Lamb Has Been Sacrificed

"Get rid of the old yeast, so that you may be a new unleavened batch—as you really are. For Christ, our Passover lamb, has been sacrificed." 1 Corinthians 5:7

This was the order of the Passover ordinance. On the 10th day of Abib, each household selected and isolated a lamb without defect. On the 14th day between two evenings, the lamb was sacrificed. They took blood from the lamb and smeared it on the doorframes of their houses. They barbecued the lamb and ate it with bitter herbs and unleavened bread. The same night God's angel killed the firstborns of the Egyptians and spared the firstborns of the Israelites.

God ordered the Israelites to celebrate this ordinance as a memorial of their redemption from slavery, and as a pointer to Christ who would be slain centuries later to redeem men from the slavery of sin and eternal death.

Christ restricted his movements some days close to his crucifixion. He was arrested as the Jews prepared for the Passover. On Passover day, he was crucified, he was offered a bitter cup of wine mixed with myrrh and he died at twilight. He was the ultimate Passover lamb.

After Christ's Crucifixion, the Passover changed. We now break bread and share a cup of wine to commemorate our redemption from sin and death through Christ's death on the cross.

Prayers:

....

....

....

....

Get Rid of the Old Leaven of Wickedness

"Get rid of the old yeast, so that you may be a new unleavened batch—as you really are. For Christ, our Passover lamb, has been sacrificed. Therefore let us keep the Festival, not with the old bread leavened with malice and wickedness, but with the unleavened bread of sincerity and truth."

The Passover was immediately followed by a week-long festival of unleavened bread. It started on the 15th day of Abib up to the 21st day of Abib. The first day and the last day of the week were God's Sabbaths.

During this week, the Hebrews took unleavened bread to remember the night they ate unleavened bread as they left Egypt in haste. They ritually lit lamps and searched for remains of leaven in their houses and swept them away.

We have been justified through the death of our Passover lamb and we have become new sincere and truthful creatures in Him. We now need to continually assess our lives for the presence of the old leaven of malice and wickedness and get rid of it.

Search me, God, and know my heart; test me and know my anxious thoughts. See if there is any offensive way in me, and lead me in the way everlasting.

Prayers:

....
....
....
....
....

Pentecost

"When the day of Pentecost came, they were all together in one place."
Acts 2:1

Also called the Feast of Weeks as it came seven weeks after the Passover. It was a Sabbath after the harvest when the Israelites were required to appear before the Lord in Jerusalem with a freewill offering, rejoicing and thankful to him for the harvest.

Seven weeks after Christ ascended, disciples gathered in Jerusalem and waited for the baptism of the holy spirit. They had sold their goods and possessions and committed the proceeds to the work of preaching the gospel. This was their freewill offering.

Led by the Holy Spirit, Peter preached and three thousand souls were added to the fold that day. This was the harvest from Christ's work of three and half years. This harvest was a precursor of the great harvest that will take place before Christ returns.

Through our free will offerings, let's support the work of sowing the good seed of the gospel.

We will need a double measure of God's spirit that was poured at Pentecost.

Prayers:

....
....
....
....
....
....

The Sanctuary

The initial ark was a beautiful, tent-like structure measuring 15 feet by 45 feet, based on an 18-inch cubit. The walls consisted of upright wooden boards placed in silver sockets and covered with a layer of gold (Exodus 26:15–19, 29). The roof was composed of four layers: linen, goat hair, ram skin, and badger skin (Exodus 26:1, 7–14). Inside, there were two rooms: the Holy Place and the Most Holy Place. These rooms were separated by a thick, weighty veil or curtain. Surrounding the sanctuary was a courtyard, spanning an area of 75 feet by 150 feet *(Exodus 27:18)*. This courtyard was enclosed by a fine linen cloth supported by 60 brass pillars

(Exodus 27:9–16).

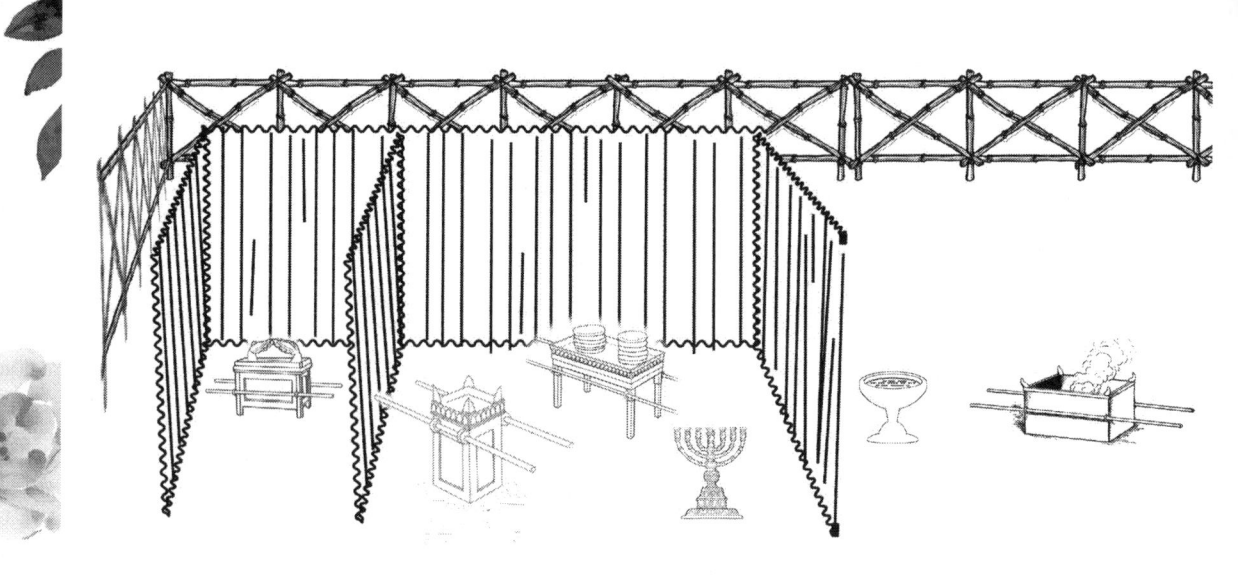

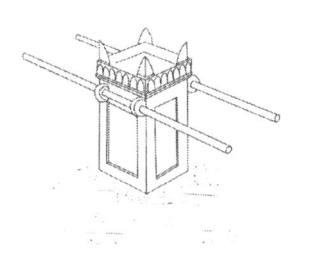

Altar of Incense

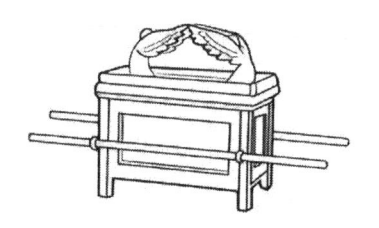

Ark of the Covenant

Lampstand

Altar of Sacrifice

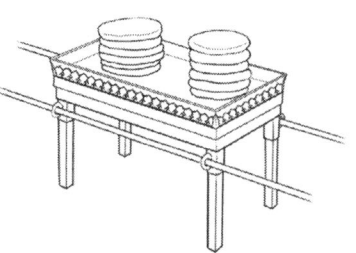

Table of Showbread

Lavar

Note: items not drawn to scale

The Ark of the Covenant

Read Exodus 25:10–22

This was a box in the holy of holies containing the stone tablets upon which God engraved his holy laws. The cover of the box was called the mercy seat. It had gold-beaten cherubim on either side facing the law in the ark.

The law is like a mirror that points out our transgressions. The mercy seat represents God's throne of mercy where all repentant sinners obtain mercy and pardon for their sins and are saved from the requirements of the law.

The golden cherubim symbolizes the covering cherubim surrounding God's throne in heaven.

Prayers:

The Altar of Incense

Read Exodus 30:1–8

This was a golden altar that was positioned before the veil in the holy place. On the altar was a bowl-like golden crown where priests placed incense that burnt day and night filling the holy place with perfume.

The priest officiating in the holy place represents Christ who now ministers in the heavenly sanctuary interceding for us. Day and night, He receives the prayers of his children and mingles them with incense before presenting them to God.

"In the same way, the Spirit helps us in our weakness. We do not know what we ought to pray for, but the Spirit himself intercedes for us through wordless groans. And he who searches our hearts knows the mind of the Spirit because the Spirit intercedes for God's people in accordance with the will of God." Romans 6:26-27

Prayers:

....
....
....
....
....
....
....
....

The Menora

"You are the light of the world. A town built on a hill cannot be hidden. Neither do people light a lamp and put it under a bowl. Instead, they put it on its stand, and it gives light to everyone in the house. In the same way, let your light shine before others, that they may see your good deeds and glorify your Father in heaven." Matthew 5:14-16, Read Exodus 25:31–32, 37–40; 26:35

Menorah was a golden candlestick with seven golden lamps. It was positioned in the southern part of the holy place. Morning and evening, the priest ministered in the holy place to trim the lamps and keep them burning.

Christians are God's candlestick bearing the lamps that will light the moral darkness of our time. When they lift Christ through their lives and efforts, many will be drawn to God's kingdom.

Let's pray for the power of the holy spirit to help us be effective light bearers.

Prayers:

....
....
....
....
....
....
....

The Table of Showbread

"I am the living bread which came down from heaven. If anyone eats of this bread, he will live forever; and the bread that I shall give is My flesh, which I shall give for the life of the world." John 6:51, Read Exodus 25:23, 29–30; 26:35

This was a golden table that stood at the northern side of the holy place. Every Sabbath, priests prepared twelve pieces of unleavened bread and placed them on the table arranged in two stacks of six each. After a week, the bread was consumed and replaced by the priests.

When Christians will feed on His word, it has life-giving power and it will wean their affections of this world.

As Christians, we depend on God for our physical and spiritual nourishment through Christ our mediator.

Every sabbath, when we rest from our Labors and attend worship service, we're renewed when we feed from his word. This gives us the energy to serve him through the week.

Prayers:

....
....
....
....
....
....
....

The Lavar

Read Exodus 30:17–21

This was a brazen vessel that stood between the altar of sacrifice and the door of the sanctuary. Priests washed their hands in the laver before performing any service in the sanctuary. Failure to wash hands by the priests was punished by death.

The laver and the hand-washing routine were to impress upon the Israelites that God demands purity and holiness from His people.

Except a man be born of water and the spirit, he will not enter the Kingdom of God

Prayers:

....
....
....
....
....
....
....
....
....
....
....

The Altar of Burnt Offering

Read Exodus 27:1–8; 30:18

This furniture was a hollow box made out of wood and overlaid with brass. It had four brass horns, one on each corner. It had a mesh of brass at the center to hold the fire and allow ash to drop below.

The fire of the altar was started by God and burned day and night and was never to be extinguished.

Fire represented God's judgment. The sacrifice upon the altar represented sin. The fire of God will burn continually in our lives until sin is destroyed.

The wages of sin is death. The innocent animal was killed instead of the sinner. This pointed to Calvary where Christ died as a sacrifice for sin. He was the ultimate sacrifice that burned on the brazen altar of sacrifice to reconcile humanity to God.

It was a place of forgiveness. The innocent animal was killed and burnt while the guilty sinner walked away from the altar free from sin.

Prayers:

Lessons From Mt. Sinai & More

Let Go of Past Hurts

"Do not mistreat or oppress a foreigner, for you were foreigners in Egypt."
Exodus 22:21

The Israelites suffered greatly in Egypt. They did not have freedom, they were not treated with dignity, they labored hard but they did not have money to meet their basic needs, and they were second-class citizens who were constantly looked down upon.

God knew his people looked back to their past with bitterness. He warned them not to use their painful past against the foreigners in Canaan.

God expected the more privileged Israelites to show compassion to the less fortunate and offer them moral, financial and material support.

We were all slaves in sin until God saved us. Let us remember we were saved unto good works. By this, everyone will know you love me by loving one another.

Prayers:

....
....
....
....
....
....
....
....

God of Justice and Mercy

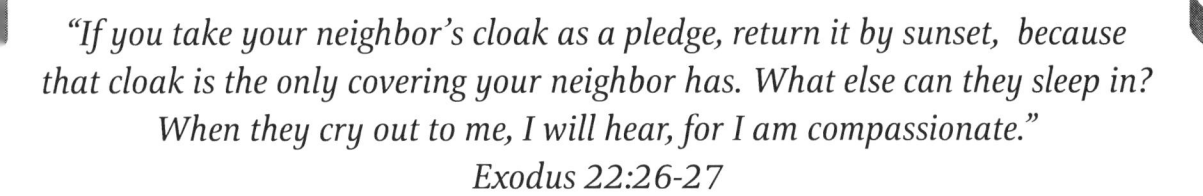

"If you take your neighbor's cloak as a pledge, return it by sunset, because that cloak is the only covering your neighbor has. What else can they sleep in? When they cry out to me, I will hear, for I am compassionate."
Exodus 22:26-27

God was opposed to slavery. But because the practice existed, he gave legislation to safeguard the rights and liberties of slaves. The laws guarded families of slaves against disruption. The laws to some extent protected slaves against maltreatment and permanent enslavement.

Restitution for loss or injury ensured the perpetrators compensate the victims for the loss incurred. Restitution also served to punish and educate the offender and deter against repeat offenses.

Gleaning provided an opportunity for the landless with means to support themselves and their families.

Legislation ensured fair and just transactions between lenders and borrowers. It discouraged prohibitive interest rates and collateral. For instance, a man who put his coat as collateral should get it back at night to protect him against the cold. Lenders should not perpetuate destitution.

Prayers:

....
....
....
....
....

Agreement Sealed in Blood

"Moses then took the blood, sprinkled it on the people and said, "This is the blood of the covenant that the Lord has made with you in accordance with all these words." Exodus 24:8

Moses read the Book of the Covenant to the Israelites and they all responded and said, "Everything the Lord has said we will do." On the altar he built at the foot of the mountain, young Israelite men offered burnt offerings, and sacrificed young bulls as peace offerings unto the Lord.

He took half of the blood in bowls and sprinkled it on the altar of sacrifice, he also took the other half he sprinkled it on the people and told them this is the blood that seals the covenant of the Lord I have read to you.

After the covenant was sealed by the blood, Moses, Aaron, Nadab, Abihu and the seventy elders went up to the mountain. They saw God on a sapphire pavement and had fellowship with him without the consequence of death.

During the last supper, Jesus presented the cup to his disciples and said, "Drink from it, all of you. This is my blood of the covenant, which is poured out for many for the forgiveness of sins."

Through the blood, sinful man is reconciled to God.

Prayers:

....
....
....
....

Urim and Thummim

"You shall put in the breastpiece of judgment the Urim and the Thummim, and they shall be over Aaron's heart when he goes in before the Lord; and Aaron shall carry the judgment of the sons of Israel over his heart before the Lord continually." Exodus 28:30

At some point, David called the priest to bring an ephod when he wanted to establish God's will on an issue. When Joshua took over leadership from Moses, he was instructed to depend on the revelation of Urim through Eleazer the high priest.

Urim and Thummim were two bright stones that were hidden within the breastplate, one on either side. They were placed close to the high priest's heart and were used to determine God's will on matters brought to the priest.

Before we pursue any matter, big or small, it is important to determine whether it is permissible in God's eyes.

Through the study of the scriptures and prayers, Christians have the means to establish God's will. God is willing and ready to provide answers to the questions we put to him.

Prayers:

....

....

....

....

....

....

Ear, Thumb and Big Toe

"Take the other ram, and Aaron and his sons shall lay their hands on its head. Slaughter it, take some of its blood and put it on the lobes of the right ears of Aaron and his sons, on the thumbs of their right hands, and the big toes of their right feet. Then splash blood against the sides of the altar."
Exodus 29:19-20

In consecrating the priests for the Tabernacle ministry, the blood from a Ram was smeared to the particular members of their bodies: The right ear, the thumb of the right hand and the toe of the right foot. It denoted the complete dedication of the priest to God's ministry in their hearing, conduct and walk.

Pray and purpose to only listen to what honors and glorifies God. The Lord is ready to anoint your thumbs and make you an instrument to do his will and serve his people within your circle of influence. God desires that his servants walk uprightly, follow Christ's footsteps and enlist many to the coming Kingdom.

Like Christ, our meat as Christians should be to do God's will through what we hear, through our service to humanity and in our spiritual walk (John 3:34).

Prayers:

....
....
....
....
....
....
....

Skill Up

"Then the Lord said to Moses, "See, I have chosen Bezalel son of Uri, the son of Hur, of the tribe of Judah, and I have filled him with the Spirit of God, with wisdom, with understanding, with knowledge and with all kinds of skills"
Exodus 31:1-3

Science, art and engineering were enablers of Egyptian civilization. God wanted the Israelites to learn and benefit from this environment and be prepared to start, build and advance their Kingdom in Canaan.

Even at the height of their slavery, not every Hebrew was involved in brick-making. Some were in formal employment like Shifra and Puah. Yet some like Bezaleel and Aholiab were highly learned and trained in sophisticated trades like jewelry, metalwork, carpentry, weaving, dying and embroidery among others.

God filled Bezalel and Aholiab with the Holy Spirit, who made them more zealous and innovative and increased their capacity to supervise, teach others and interpret the intricate plan of constructing the sanctuary.

We now need to level up our abilities and acquire a skill and another. We will become better suited to serve God in his vineyard.

Prayers:

....
....
....
....
....
....
....

Choose God's Honor over Man's Approval

"For they loved human praise more than praise from God" John 12:43
Exodus 32:23-24

Aaron knew God had forbidden idol worship when He gave the ten commandments in Exodus chapter 20. As a leader, he failed the responsibility test when he gave in to the people's pressure and helped cast and mold a golden calf for their worship. People were greatly plagued as a consequence of worshiping the golden calf.

Leaders or individuals must know God's will and be committed to obeying God rather than man. They should not allow the spirit of fear to dictate their decisions.

Prayers:

Own Up Aaron

"Do not be angry, my lord," Aaron answered. "You know how prone these people are to evil. They said to me, 'Make us gods who will go before us. As for this fellow Moses who brought us up out of Egypt, we don't know what has happened to him.' So I told them, 'Whoever has any gold jewelry, take it off.' Then they gave me the gold, and I threw it into the fire, and out came this calf!" Exodus 32:22-24

When Adam and Eve sinned and God came to look for them, they had a golden opportunity to express their remorse and repent but they did not. Adam blamed Eve and Eve blamed the serpent.

When Moses descended from Mount Sinai and asked Aaron to account for the golden calf making and worship, Aaron exonerated himself and blamed his fellow Israelites for the sin.

I find Aaron's response funny: "They gave me gold and I threw it into the fire and out came this calf!". But the truth Aaron carefully molded the molten gold into the golden calf.

When we are guilty of sin, and the holy spirit points us to our transgression, we will do well not to excuse our sin by blaming others or circumstances. Let us own up the sin and seek God's mercies (1 John 1:9).

Prayers:

....

....

....

....

Are You on the Lord's Side?

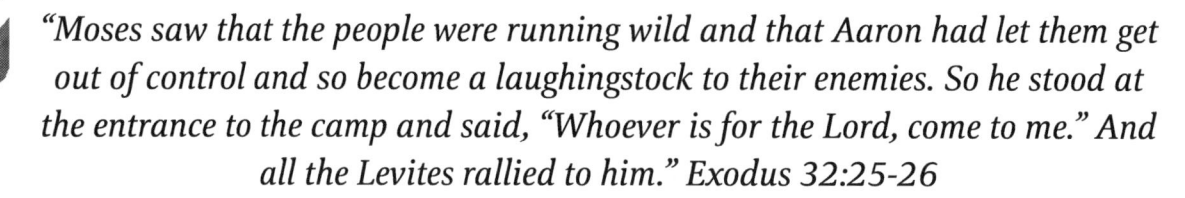

"Moses saw that the people were running wild and that Aaron had let them get out of control and so become a laughingstock to their enemies. So he stood at the entrance to the camp and said, "Whoever is for the Lord, come to me." And all the Levites rallied to him." Exodus 32:25-26

Moses descended from Mount Sinai and met with the disheartening scenes of apostasy in the camp. People were shouting, dancing, rioting and worshiping the golden calf Aaron had made for them. He stood at the entrance of the camp and made a call that simply said, "Whoever is for the Lord, come to me".

This was an invitation to repentance. It was an opportunity for those in the mob who felt genuinely remorseful for what had happened to step out and join the Lord's side. It was only the Levites who hearkened to the call and came forth.

Those who chose to remain in the mob had made a choice not to be on the Lord's side. Then Moses ordered the Levites each to strap a sword to himself, sweep through the camp, and without fear or favor execute judgment on God's behalf. About three thousand people were massacred on that day.

Prayers:

....
....
....
....
....
....
....

Prayer of a Righteous Woman

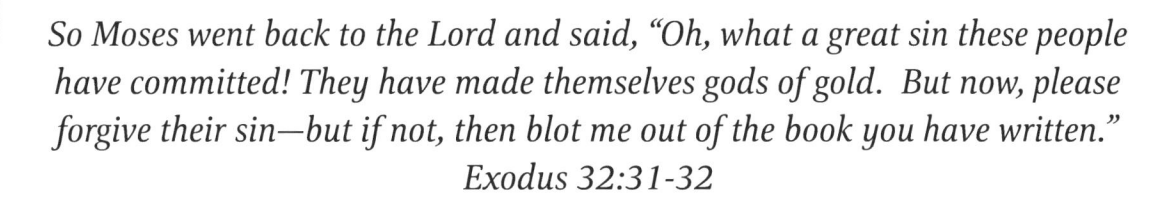

So Moses went back to the Lord and said, "Oh, what a great sin these people have committed! They have made themselves gods of gold. But now, please forgive their sin—but if not, then blot me out of the book you have written."
Exodus 32:31-32

The children of Jacob had sinned. God threatened to kill them all and raise another generation through Moses, His friend. Moses turned down this offer and decided to take advantage of this relationship and intercede for his kinsmen.

It took the sacrifice of God's begotten son - in whom he is well pleased - for the human race to be reconciled to Himself.

We need intercessors who are God's friends to unlock His mercies and grace for us. Each day is an opportunity to walk right with our Creator and cultivate friendship. And when we are called to intercede for our brethren, God will hear our fervent prayers and bring relief.

"Confess your faults one to another, and pray one for another, that ye may be healed. The effectual fervent prayer of a righteous man availeth much"

Prayers:

....
....
....
....
....

Time in the Closet Watching & Praying

" The LORD would speak to Moses face to face, as one speaks to a friend. Then Moses would return to the camp, but his young aide Joshua son of Nun did not leave the tent."
Exodus 33:11

These moments in the tent brought a lasting impact on Joshua's life. Joshua together with Caleb, out of the twelve spies, brought a report of faith about Canaan. In the book of Joshua, we meet a strong and courageous young man who was ready to fit into Moses' big shoes of leadership and cross the Israelites through the Jordan River to Canaan.

Israelites apostatised when Moses was on Mount Sinai, they made a golden calf and bowed down to it. God was angry and He threatened to kill all the Israelites except Moses or withdraw his presence from them and leave them on their own.

Moses removed the tent of meeting from within the camp and pitched it without the camp. Whenever Moses entered the tent to pray, God would come down in the form of a pillar of cloud that stood at the entrance of the tent. Moses could speak to God as a man speaks to a friend. He sought God to forgive the Israelites and stay his judgements against them.

After these sessions with God, Moses could leave the tent. The Bible says Joshua, an aid to Moses, remained in the tent having devotion to God.

Joshua, though a young man, understood the crisis and the cloud of judgment that hung on their heads. He added to Moses' efforts and tarried in the tent praying and interceding on behalf of his kinsmen. God answered their prayers.

Jesus instructed us to watch and pray. Like his friends in the garden of Gethsemane, we easily surrender to sleep and lethargy because our bodies are weak. We risk being overtaken by temptation, if we don't pray.

Let's tarry in our closets, keep watch and pray.

Prayers:

The Power of Persistent Prayer

"Elijah was a human being, even as we are. He prayed earnestly that it would not rain, and it did not rain on the land for three and a half years." James 5:17

Moses proved a faithful intercessor for his kinsmen. When they sinned by worshiping the golden calf and God threatened to kill them all, Moses put up a very strong case against the idea, and God heard him.

In obtaining their forgiveness, Moses fasted for forty days and nights. He was willing to have his name blotted out of the Book of Life unless God forgave the Israelites.

When God expressed his interest to withdraw his presence from the camp, Moses implored God to consider his position.

He stood his ground and told God, we will not move an inch toward Canaan without you. God changed his position and accompanied the Hebrews on their journey.

Prayers:

....
....
....
....
....
....
....

God's Character

"The Lord, the Lord, the compassionate and gracious God, slow to anger, abounding in love and faithfulness, maintaining love to thousands, and forgiving wickedness, rebellion and sin. Yet he does not leave the guilty unpunished; he punishes the children and their children for the sin of the parents to the third and fourth generation." Exodus 34:6

The Lord revealed His character to Moses. The Lord is merciful; he sympathizes with our weakness and troubles. He's very patient and willing to show His love to thousands of people. He's faithful to His promises and there's no variableness with Him.

He's also just and will hold individuals accountable for their sins. The Bible says in Ezekiel 18: 20 "The soul who sins is the one who will die. The son will not share the guilt of the father, nor will the father share the guilt of the son."

The other uncomfortable truth in the passage is that children are more likely to repeat the sins of their parents.

We can trust God to help us overcome the evil tendencies handed over to us by our past generation.

Prayers:

....
....
....
....

Our Children May Harvest the Consequences of Our Actions

" And he passed in front of Moses, proclaiming, "The Lord, the Lord, the compassionate and gracious God, slow to anger, abounding in love and faithfulness, maintaining love to thousands, and forgiving wickedness, rebellion and sin. Yet he does not leave the guilty unpunished; he punishes the children and their children for the sin of the parents to the third and fourth generation." Exodus 34:6

This verse looked at from another standpoint, has a message to parents. It is in their hands to influence posterity either positively or negatively. Parents ought to be deliberate and conscious in curating the traits they will transmit to their children.

If you're a victim of inherited negative influences, like Hezekiah and Josiah who were children of idolaters, you have a golden opportunity to rework the future.
Let's pray to God to work in us a character that is worthy of transmitting to the future generation.

Prayers:

....
....
....
....
....
....
....
....

The Path to True Generosity: Unveiling the Principles of Giving

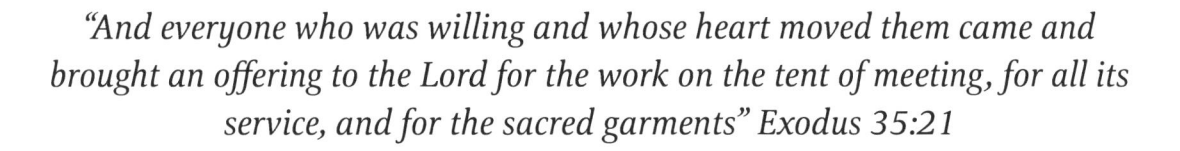

"And everyone who was willing and whose heart moved them came and brought an offering to the Lord for the work on the tent of meeting, for all its service, and for the sacred garments" Exodus 35:21

People gave from what they had. God bestows his gifts to us from which we are to contribute towards his work. The ex-slaves still had the wealth they had plundered from the Egyptians on the eve of their escape.

God loves a cheerful giver. Everyone retreated to their tent, and as the spirit moved them, they willingly decided what to present to the lord. None should give under compulsion.

People gave according to their ability. The princes gave the costly precious stones and the choicest spices for incense. Some gave the silver and brass metals while others gave the acacia wood. Those who could not contribute materially contributed through the services of free labor.

They gave more materials than required. Israelites manifested generosity in their giving, they continued to bring their gifts until they were restrained. We're to bring tithes and offerings so there is plenty in God's storehouse.

Prayers:

....

....

....

....

Diligent and Selfless Coworkers

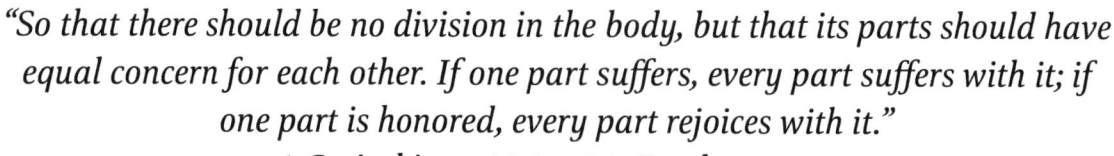

"So that there should be no division in the body, but that its parts should have equal concern for each other. If one part suffers, every part suffers with it; if one part is honored, every part rejoices with it."
1 Corinthians 12:25-26, Exodus 36:1-2

God appointed two Hebrew men and filled them with wisdom to lead the project of building the sanctuary. Bezaleel, from the tribe of Judah, was the chief designer while Aholiab, from the tribe of Dan, was his second-in-command.

The zeal, activity and mannerisms they exhibited while dispensing their duties were remarkable. They rose above selfish interests and tribal rivalry and joined hands as friends in doing God's work.

The one with lesser gifts gladly served in their capacity and was not envious of the one with greater.

They remained united and ensured once the work started, it never stopped until the sanctuary was completed.

Such spirit is needed in our churches and organizations. By embracing diversity, we should work together to edify the bodies, organizations or institutions where we serve.

Prayers:

....
....
....
....
....

Women Donated Brass Mirrors

"They made the bronze basin and its bronze stand from the mirrors of the women who served at the entrance to the tent of meeting." Exodus 38:8

Like Mary of Bethany who anointed Christ's feet with expensive oil from an alabaster box(Mat 26:7), this is another example of women expressing their devotion to God through acts of sacrifice.

Through the donation of their treasured mirrors, they expressed gratitude to God for saving them from slavery and his intentions to settle them in the promised land.

Redeemed women are empowered not to withhold a thing that will serve God and humanity. The homeless will find refuge in their homes, and the destitute will feed from the bounties of their tables. They are always seeking opportunities to share joy and happiness with people by doing good.

Prayers:

....
....
....
....
....
....
....
....
....

Good Stewardship Is Exemplified by Accountability

"These are the amounts of the materials used for the tabernacle, the tabernacle of the covenant law, which were recorded at Moses' command by the Levites under the direction of Ithamar son of Aaron, the priest." Exodus 38:21

When the construction of the Sanctuary was finished, Moses ordered the Levites led by Ithamar, the son of Aaron, to enumerate the metals they had used.

The enumeration was done and the report was shared to the Hebrews who through their giving sponsored the project. This was good stewardship.

When leaders are accountable for the financial and material resources entrusted to them, it engenders trust in their leadership, motivates giving, shields them against accusations of embezzlement and checks against wastages.

Prayers:

....
....
....
....
....
....
....
....
....

God is Holy

"Holy, holy, holy is the Lord Almighty; the whole earth is full of his glory."
Isaiah 6:3

The book Exodus highlights God's holy, pure and sinless nature. Israelites were required to consecrate themselves for two days and wash their garments before meeting God at Mount Sinai.

The burning bush, thunder, lightning or pillar of cloud and other signs that represented God's presence punctuated God's character of holiness.

The ten commandments are a mirror of God's holy character.

The holy of holies in the Sanctuary was a compartment where God dwelt among his people. It required a consecrated high priest to access God in this compartment once a year to atone for the sins of the Israelites. Those with unrepented sins at the end of the atonement ordinance were cut off.

These and many other instances in the Bible contrast sinful human character against God's holy character. God's holiness demands that sin is punished.

We have all sinned and fallen short of God's glory (Rom 3:23). We need the merits of Christ's perfect life to unlock the treasures of mercy from God. For the love of humanity, Christ was treated as we deserve so we are treated as He deserves.

Prayers:

....

....

....

Human Nature

"Be always on the watch, and pray that you may be able to escape all that is about to happen and that you may be able to stand before the Son of Man."
Luke 21:36

God had lofty plans for the Israelites. He wanted to mold them to be peculiar and holy people, a nation of priests through whom he would reach the entire universe with His saving grace.

But the frailties of human nature had the best of them. They loved themselves more than they Loved God. They loved the miracles more than the miracle worker.

Despite God's grace and mercies, they continued being unholy, unthankful, headstrong and lacking self-control.

God's laws and tokens of judgment did not arouse them to righteousness.

A journey that should have taken two weeks to complete took them forty years.

It is through prayer we'll be able to rise above carnal inclinations and be fit for the heavenly Kingdom.

Prayers:

....
....
....
....
....

Egypt Is a Precursor

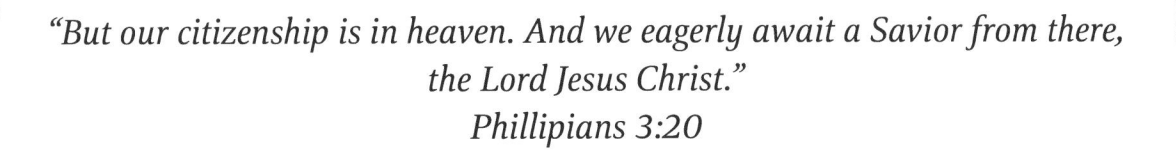

"But our citizenship is in heaven. And we eagerly await a Savior from there, the Lord Jesus Christ."
Phillipians 3:20

Egypt is an object lesson for Christians. It was a place of refuge from famine before it degenerated into a place of affliction and bondage.

While this world could afford temporary luxury and comfort, Christians should not be lulled to think it is our abiding city.

In the same way, Hebrews were aliens in Egypt, Christians are pilgrims, and Heaven is their Canaan. God owns the universe but Satan and his taskmasters have gained control, and have made men laborers and slaves in sin.

Like God sent Moses to deliver Jews from bondage, He has sent His son to deliver men from slavery of sin and the curse of eternal death

Prayers:

....

....

....

....

....

....

....

....

Printed in Great Britain
by Amazon